Am I Disciplined?

By

Evangelist Shonya Hattley

Dorrance Publishing Co
585 Alpha Drive
Suite 103
Pittsburgh, PA 15238
Visit our website at www.dorrancebookstore.com

ISBN:979-8-88683-386-7
eISBN:979-8-88683-365-2

Introduction

My purpose for this book is to encourage all who read this book to know that God will strengthen you. May the anointing of God flow as he allows me to minister and witness to many. May this book guide you to understanding who God is and may you grow in maturity in your walk with Jesus Christ. May these words inspire you as you cope with your peers daily. May God's will alone be done in your lives daily. It is important that we surrender totally to him, giving our life, our thoughts, our plans, and our visions and dreams to him, whatever our journey will be that God has destined for us. Amen!

Intermission Self-Disciplined: A Gem Thought Self-Disciplined

May your thoughts be positive, which will create a sweet atmosphere about your surroundings. Negative thoughts will create ruin and disaster! What a man thinketh in his heart, so is he. (Proverbs 23:7). May your thoughts become pure. May your ambitions reach your God given plans and purpose for your life. If you think negatively you will never better yourself to move forward in life. Don't let ruin and disaster be a great waste in your life!

This book as God inspired me to write, under his guidance, by humbling me, enabling me to grow spiritually unto maturity in him. Through manifold trials, God counseled me to know what it really means to become disciplined. God's hand was and is still heavy upon me in his defining terms of what discipline means. One must believe God. One must become an obedient listener. One must have the heart and desire to be willing to change. One must refrain his/her self to letting go and to trust God in the process of being self-controlled, although God's plan is for us to examine ourselves with conviction under the auction of the Holy Ghost. Let God be Lord over our lives!

I pray that you will be wholly blameless and enriched through Jesus Christ. I pray that you will grow closer to him as we see the days quickly approaching. I pray that the chains of darkness be destroyed in your lives under God's anointing! May God continue to strengthen you in his love, wisdom, knowledge, and understanding! May God Richly Bless You!

Galatians 2:20: I am crucified with Christ; Nevertheless I live; yet not I but Christ liveth in me; and the life which I now live in the flesh. I live by faith in the Son of God, who loved me and gave himself for me. Job 36:10: He also opened their ear to discipline and commandeth that they return from iniquity.

Chapter One: Self-Discipline

This is an area; we as human beings quite struggle with in our lives daily. How? In so many ways; our motives, our characters, our level of tolerance, and how we are able to respond to having to control our actions. This is a hard thing to do, we depend on others to motivate us, we rely on other opinions instead of seeking the face of God. We must look at ourselves to have a desire to do what is the best thing to do. We must make some adjustments along the way. We should learn how to create healthy lifestyles for ourselves, along with family, friends and our fellow Christians.

We must become devoted to making rightful decisions and be willing to overcome our weakness to break the barriers that are holding us back from performing and reaching the task. We have to prioritize to reach our goals. Stay on guard and be willing to admit to your problems. Find ways to overcome them with a good solution. May God lead you to a positive influence that will show you spiritual support. Although we have to quite often remind ourselves to put this or that under control, at the end there are consequences for our actions. Sometimes you have to punish yourself to restrain from causing mishaps in your life. Break away from bad habits, do not engage in wrong influences whether it's from childhood friends all the way until now. Restrain yourself from certain foods, alcohol, making illegal money, greed, coveting, and having uncontrolled wants which leads to unhappiness, depression, confusion, and despair.

In John 5:30, Jesus illustrates how he could do nothing of his own. He had to be willing to hear the Father's instructions for righteous judgment to what is right. GOD who is JUST. Jesus did not come to the Earth to do his own will, but the will of the Father which sent him!

John 5:30: I can of my own self do nothing as I hear, I judge; and my judgment is just because I seek not my own will, but the will of the Father which hath sent me.

We must have this same demonstration in our daily lives to become disciplined. We cannot do anything on our own. We must seek God's perfect will to be willing to say, "Enough is Enough " in our lives that we can overcome any hindrance that will keep us from moving forward! We must become an attentive listener to be willing to follow sound instructions from God. We must submit to him in his authoritative word as God speaks to us how we ought to live. This is how we can overcome these obstacles that seem to stand in our way!
I would like to enlighten you on the key elements how we can overcome daily:

1. Learn to appreciate yourself, do not look for approval of men, but GOD totally.
2. Knowing that you are precious in the sight of God. Psalms 139:14: I will praise thee for I am fearfully and wonderfully made; marvelous are thy works; and that my soul knoweth right well.
3. Let not depression or stress tend to hover over you.
4. Be willing to adapt to changes so you can overcome hardships
5. Learn to let go of past hurts, rejection and fears.
6. Love and embrace yourself so healing can be your strongest weapons from the dark deep wounds that were covered for so long.
7. Forgive, Forgive, Forgive.
8. Become a positive thinker and cancel all negativity.
9. Start new and adapt to changes that will be good for progress.

How else can I define my personal self to be under control?

1 Corinthians 9:27 (KJV) But I keep under my body and bring it into subjection: lest that by any means, when I have preached to others I myself should be a castaway.

I must lay myself aside and put it under control and not let any corruptible thing enter into my house (Spiritual) meaning my body which is the temple of the HOLY GHOST. I must not let myself be the authority to rule or to contaminate my physical body. I must with God's help not to harm myself nor others. I must become obedient to preach the Gospel as God instructed the Apostle Paul to do so, you and I. The Apostle Paul states in God's word is to give us clarity what God says we must do as Christians and Leaders. We must have a desire to put our body under subjection with total submission unto God and learn to say "NO" to temptations when they seem to lurk unaware in our lives. Amen!

How can we as Christians hear God's voice? and to know when he is Speaking? Here are several Scriptures on Obedience and hearing God's voice. God calls his sheep by name. John 10:3-5 (KJV)3) To him the Porter openeth; and the sheep hear his voice; and he calleth his own sheep by name, and leadeth them out. 4) And when he putteth forth his own sheep, he goeth before them, and the sheep follow him; for they know his voice. 5) And a stranger will not follow but will flee from him: for they know not the voice of strangers.

Another word for discipline is chasten. Hebrews 12:5-7 describes the chastening from God on how he corrects us and to turn from the wrong doings and corrects us as individuals because he loves us so much. Here you will find these encouraging scriptures.

Hebrews 12:5: And ye have forgotten the exhortation which speaketh unto you as unto children. My son despise not thou the chastening of the LORD, Nor faint when thou are rebuked of him. 6) For whom the Lord loveth he chasteneth and scourgeth every son whom he receiveth. 7) If ye endure chastening, God dealeth with you as with sons for what son is he whom the father chasteneth not?

Psalm 94:12: Blessed is the man whom thou chastenest O LORD and teaches him out of thy law. Deuteronomy 8:5: Thou shalt also consider in thine heart, that as a man chasteneth his son, so the LORD thy God chasteneth thee.

Also, to become self-disciplined requires action and investment in it has a purpose and value of individuality to be willing to do what is right. It is important to put off procrastination and put on the "I can" attitude from start to finish. Self-discipline is when one should make a commitment to overcome barriers, weights, and hindrances from reaching your visions and plans in your life. It is important to have a focused mindset so you can accomplish the areas you need to overcome.

Chapter Two: Self-Disciplined

Self-Disciplined In Leadership:

A. Self-discipline means one must restrict itself from things that will cause hindrance.

B. In order for one to become effective in leadership, we must seek and yield all things to God. This process includes both natural and spiritual responsibilities. It is important that leaders must set aside differences, habits and issues to God. Cease from unhealthy fleshly appetites that will cause major mishaps in life.

C. Devote yourself having rightful posture in meeting and completing tasks.

D. Avoid procrastination

E. You must become effective in both positive structure and fundamental attitudes in having good characteristics in Jesus Christ. How? To lead, to teach, and to counsel with bible- based contents. You must have a dedicated prayer life and essential to be obedient in the calling of Jesus Christ.

F. You must admit to making mistakes and be willing to change one's ways and mindset to find healthy ways to do better.

G. Become motivated to adapt to changes in life, peers, and social affairs

H. Become dramatic (vivid, strong, active, exciting, bright). A positive resource to become a powerful voice to take a stand for Christ; an ambassador for Jesus Christ.

Quite often, I've seen and experienced what hardships leaders had to put their life on the line to sacrifice everything for the church of Jesus Christ. Many endure pain, hurt, and counseling for numerous hours with people. Many have a heart for God's people and people have taken advantage of their roles as leaders in the Church. Some have endured jealousy, competition, and struggles both inside and outside of the Church among God's people. But this is how true leadership is in order to reign with Jesus Christ, especially those who are after God's own heart. Just imagine a true man or woman of God had to endure hardships to become effective in partaking in the sufferings of Christ. If they so persecuted Christ, they likewise will do the same to true leadership.

The question is, am I self-disciplined? Am I independent? How can I find healing and peace within? Galatians 5:24 Amplified Bible 24 And those who belong to Christ Jesus have crucified the [a]sinful nature together with its passions and appetites.

Chapter Three: Self-Disciplined in the Church

In this chapter is an important essential part of how effective the church must be and to apply ourselves to become disciplined. Our conversation must be chasten with Godly fear and consideration for one another. Jesus Christ made it clear in his mission and earthy ministry as it is self-explained in Matthew 16:18(Amplified Bible): 18 And I say to you that you are [a]Peter, and on this [b]rock I will build My church; and the [c]gates of Hades (death) will not overpower it [by preventing the resurrection of the Christ].

This explains end times and even so now, God is setting his church in order and he has given us the keys how we must live, act and proclaim the Gospel of Jesus Christ as born again believers. The wheat and the tares will grow together, but the day of judgment God will separate them . So we must be honest and true to ourselves and to God. Who are we really serving? Is it the TRUE GOD or A God or man? Is it material possession, idolatry, witchcraft, or self-righteousness?

How is discipline in the church, as many members should be in one body of Jesus Christ is relevant? Each person is important in the role of another. Every official, layman, auxiliary, leader, youth, and all ages are crucial in their part. We shall have some likeness of God and his attributes operated by the same spirit for the sake of Gospel ministry. There must be order in the Godly realm that should coincide with God's word to the body of Jesus Christ . There must be first the Head, then the body joining body parts to become connected. Without the proper head of the body then the whole body will become paralyzed.

With that being said, there must be a flow of divine order from God. How we must operate in his spirit we can become efficient to accomplish the purpose God has designed for us to do for his Kingdom. Apostle Paul made it perfectly clear as God has given him revelation on how the church ought to follow the decrees of God to move forward. This is more evidence than ever before what we as believers failed to do serving God. 1 Corinthians 12:25-27 (Amplified Bible): 25) so that there would be no division or discord in the body [that is, lack of adaptation of the parts to each other], but that the parts may have the same concern for one another. 26) And if one member suffers, all the parts share the suffering; if one member is honored, all rejoice with it. 27) Now you [collectively] are Christ's body, and individually [you are] members of it [each with his own special purpose and function].

Why are the members of the body in disarray? 1 Corinthians 14:33 (Amplified Bible): 33) for God [who is the source of their prophesying] is not a God of confusion and disorder but of peace and order. As [is the practice] in all the churches of the saints (God's people).

What will happen if we as sons of God do not partake of chastisement? Hebrews 12:8-11 (Amplified Bible): 8 Now if you are exempt from correction and without discipline, in which all [of God's children] share, then you are illegitimate children and not sons [at all]. 9 Moreover, we have had earthly fathers who disciplined us, and we submitted and respected them [for training us]; shall we not much more willingly submit to the Father of [a]spirits, and live [by learning from His discipline]? 10 For our earthly fathers disciplined us for only a short time as seemed best to them; but He disciplines us for our good, so that we may share His holiness. 11 For the time being no discipline brings joy but seems sad and painful; yet to those who have been trained by it, afterwards it yields the peaceful fruit of righteousness [right standing with God and a lifestyle and attitude that seeks conformity to God's will and purpose].

Chapter Three: Self-Disciplined of the Church

We as a body of believers must apply the same order of correction in ourselves through reconciliation with God. We must become radiant like the Son of God as he is the light of the world. Our reflection should speak for itself to a dying dark world. If we begin to accept that the process of becoming disciplined is not an overnight process, it may take countless days, weeks and years to fully understand what God is showing us in the process.

We must have a listening ear to hear the truth and to receive the truth to show us there is room for improvement. This saying is true: we must be swift to hear, slow to speak and slow to anger. Although on the other hand in the book of Job makes an interesting affirmation on hearing is a part of discipline. Job 36:10 (Amplified Bible): "He opens their ears to instruction and discipline, And commands that they return from evil. Here is another wisdom concerning how we must pay attention to learning to listen Proverbs 16:20 (Amplified Bible): He who pays attention to the word [of God] will find good, And blessed (happy, prosperous, to be admired) is he who trusts [confidently] in the Lord.

In this next area I would like to share some scriptures I pray that will help strengthen each of us, as the body of believers of Jesus Christ. Restoration must become a crucial element among us in order to heal both naturally and supernaturally.

Galatians 6:1 (Amplified Bible): Brothers, if anyone is caught in any sin, you who are spiritual [that is, you who are responsive to the guidance of the Spirit] are to restore such a person in a spirit of gentleness [not with a sense of superiority or self-righteousness], keeping a watchful eye on yourself, so that you are not tempted as well.

1 Timothy 1:19 (Amplified Bible): 19 Keep your faith [leaning completely on God with absolute trust and confidence in His guidance] and having a good conscience; for some [people] have rejected [their moral compass] and have made a shipwreck of their faith.

I would like to conclude how the church must conduct themselves in God's House. We must know God's House is called the House of Prayer. But sadly, it should not be known to become a den of thieves.

Mark 11:17 (Amplified Bible): 17 He began to teach and say to them, "Is it not written, 'My house shall be called a house of prayer for all the nations'? But you have made it a robbers' den."

1 Timothy 3:15 (Amplified Bible): 15 in case I am delayed, so that you will know how people ought to conduct themselves in the household of God, which is the church of the living God, the pillar and foundation of the truth.

Chapter Three: Self-Disciplined

Godly Duties of True Leadership: Godly duties of true leadership as it is proposed to be set in order of effectiveness in the church of Jesus Christ.

2 Timothy 3:16 (Amplified Bible): 16 All Scripture is God-breathed [given by divine inspiration] and is profitable for instruction, for conviction [of sin], for correction [of error and restoration to obedience], for training in righteousness [learning to live in conformity to God's will, both publicly and privately—behaving honorably with personal integrity and moral courage];

2 Timothy 4:5 (Amplified Bible): 5 But as for you, be clear-headed in every situation [stay calm and cool and steady], endure every hardship [without flinching], do the work of an evangelist, fulfill [the duties of] your ministry.

Titus 2:15: 15 Tell them these things. Encourage and rebuke with full authority. Let no one disregard or despise you [conduct yourself and your teaching so as to command respect].

1 Timothy 6:3 Amplified Bible (AMP): 3 If anyone teaches a different doctrine and does not agree with the sound words of our Lord Jesus Christ, and with the doctrine and teaching which is in agreement with godliness (personal integrity, upright behavior),

1 Timothy 6:4 Amplified Bible (AMP): 4 He is conceited and woefully ignorant [understanding nothing]. He has a morbid interest in controversial questions and disputes about words, which produces envy, quarrels, verbal abuse, evil suspicions,

2 Timothy 4:2 (Amplified Bible): 2 preach the word [as an official messenger]; be ready when the time is right and even when it is not

[keep your sense of urgency, whether the opportunity seems favorable or unfavorable, whether convenient or inconvenient, whether welcome or unwelcome]; correct [those who err in doctrine or behavior], warn [those who sin], exhort and encourage [those who are growing toward spiritual maturity], with inexhaustible patience and [faithful] teaching.

Chapter Four: Challenge Yourself to be Disciplined Part One

Challenge to become a willing vessel; do not cheat yourself by taking the easy route in life. On the other hand one must become the responsible opponent to be transformed independently by being confident to learn what's valuable and to appreciate the important things in life. One's desire to attain or reach to the breaking point in coming to be successful with the "I can win, win" attitude.

When I think of a motivator of one who's willing to be a disciplinarian. It reminds me of electricity that sparks from a negative and positive battery cable. If the two different components are not connected it will spark. As a disciplined person our self-esteem must be electrified to be a go getter, a self-starter to be a winner not a quitter. We must show concerns about our health, family, finance, community, workplace and social affairs. This is a thought we do not quite think about.

Am I a supporter? Am I just wasting time? Am I really accomplishing the things in my life? we must be sure to stay with the positive ideas we want to follow through. Another important factor to help is to build up self-confidence and motivation is practicing to have a ``I can do winning attitude as we will find the scripture in God's word that will be fitting for us with a "win-win attitude. So this proves that you are not alone. You have the true one, the Holy one who can give you strength in all areas in your life!

Philippians 4: 13 (Amplified Bible): 13 I can do all things [which He has called me to do] through Him who strengthens and empowers me [to fulfill His purpose—I am self-sufficient in Christ's sufficiency; I am ready for anything and equal to anything through Him who infuses me with inner strength and confident peace.]

When you exercise, as some of us do not like to do, this is vital in our health. Think of it this way, It's like going to the gym to get a good workout. There are some helpful tips that we can do to tone our shape and with proper techniques that will help us burn the calories off. Now think of a person that will go to the end to discipline one's self in all areas in their life circumstances. I would like to paint a picture here of a flow chart of what it means to have self-control.

First it starts from the head, neck, shoulder, abdomen, legs, and then feet. There are certain areas you want to trim off and lose weight. Imagine how you've planned your workout that will help regulate your stamina and energy. You will go to the mile to discipline yourself about your health, nutrition, toning exercises, change your sleep habits, and how well you endure not to become deprived. This is what a person would do to challenge one's self, right? Just have the same energy for the Spiritual desires for God to be more self-control in our fleshly nature.

Chapter Four: Challenge Yourself to be Disciplined Part Two

Having a persistent attitude of being direct, of what you desire to do, what is right. You cannot let hindrance weigh you down , you must pursue through trials, struggles and hardships that will shape you into maturity. However it is important to seek God to live a balanced life in him, to maintain endurance, and to lay aside the weight in our circumstances that so easily throws us off guard. Having a just balance in the LORD will bring all our flaws under subjection with the Holy Spirit to guide us to submission in God!

God's word promises us that we can be healed with the word "Restoration" is much needed in our lives in order to become disciplined in God. Jesus demonstrated how one's faith can make one whole due to "Restoration" to have the confidence in God!

Luke 17:19 (Amplified Bible): Jesus said to him, "Get up and go [on your way]. Your faith [your personal trust in Me and your confidence in God's power] has restored you to health."

Wow! What a mighty God we serve! We can be restored in our health to those who believe! We must be honest with ourselves to not cheat ourselves by dishonesty! I remember God shared with me during my conversion in becoming "born-again," the Lord told me the " worst thing a person can do is Lie to themselves," being truthful to ourselves can allow God to use us more and more for his kingdom that will bring Glory to him. I like to give some encouraging scriptures that will help make us think.

Proverbs 11:1 (Contemporary English Version): 11) The Lord Hates anyone who cheats but likes everyone who is honest.

Galatians 5:24 Amplified Bible (AMP): 24 And those who belong to Christ Jesus have crucified the [a]sinful nature together with its passions and appetites.

Healing Scriptures:

Proverbs 16:24 Amplified Bible (AMP): 24) Pleasant words are like a honeycomb, Sweet and delightful to the soul and healing to the body.

Jeremiah 33:6 Amplified Bible (AMP): 6) Behold, [in the restored Jerusalem] I will bring to it health and healing, and I will heal them; and I will reveal to them an abundance of peace (prosperity, security, stability) and truth.

Luke 9:11 Amplified Bible (AMP): 11) But when the crowds learned of it, they followed Him; and He welcomed them and He began talking to them about the kingdom of God, and healing those who needed to be healed.

Chapter Five: Cravings and Appetites

Our emotions have displayed a lot from childhood , adolescence and throughout our adulthood. We have developed so many personalities along the way. How? Through family, friends, employers, relationships, which has created habits of different behavioral patterns. What cravings we as humans often didn't recognize along the way. Unexplained desires that had attached itself to us that were not there from the beginning. How can this become harmful for us as leaders, parents, children, male, female, and so on.

In this paragraph I must Identify such things that we have or had attached ourselves to and there is a need to get rid of them all by letting it GO! God's word constantly tells us not to let sin reign in our mortal body, we must yield all things to him. The outer shell of a male or female can easily deceive us by:

- Love of money more than our (Creator) GOD
- Having attraction of both male and female which is not convenient
- Manipulation
- Exposure to alcohol (Excessive wants) * drugs
- Using bodily harm on ourselves * gluttonous
- Illegal ways to make money * overbearing in persons
- Domination having total control of a person or thing
- Sexual and perverted acts

Many things we are constantly at war with the flesh and the mind. We should conclude in our everyday life to discipline ourselves to say "Enough is Enough" to avoid mistakes in the future. Oftentimes we make mistakes in our life's decision making, but we must strive to want healthy habits in place of bad habits. Shall we continue living unhealthy? Shall we continue to live in these undesirable appetites? We shall have the integrity in our heart to say "NO" to these things. The Apostle John makes a bold statement that we must take heed to in God's Word.

1 John 2:16 Amplified Bible (AMP): 16 For all that is in the world—the lust and sensual craving of the flesh and the lust and longing of the eyes and the boastful pride of life [pretentious confidence in one's resources or in the stability of earthly things]—these do not come from the Father but are from the world.

Chapter Six: The War Within Us

In this chapter I would like to point out key factors of our fleshly nature that can cause a great ruin in our lives. This can be a hurting situation if we are not careful, consequences can become costly. I would like to demonstrate and call to your attention to these areas we wrestle in our human nature . We must recognize them in order to overcome them by disciplining our fleshly thoughts and actions. These charts I will display on these subjects on wars of the flesh that causes us to develop these attitudes or behaviors within ourselves:

The Wars of the Flesh:

- Unbelief (a person who denies truth)
- Anger (hostility, wrath)
- Unforgiveness (unforgiving, unrepentant)
- Judgmental (always judging, very critical)
- Disobedience (without correction)
- Sin (wrongdoing, iniquity)
- Disorder (Confusion, Commotion)
- Corruption (evil, always taking bribes)
- Bitterness (rage, slander, form of malice)
- Greed (excessive desire or want)
- Lie (false statement)
- Fornication (consensual sexual relations between more persons)
- Covet (desiring what belongs to another person)
- Lust (Strong desire of persons or thing)

Wars of the Mind:

- Negativity (expressing or responding in unpleasant way)
- Clamor (loud outcry or noise or feeling you have to be loud all the time)
- Crafty (evil schemes, deceitful)
- Cunning (a person who plots evil things)
- Devilish (wicked person, evil spirit)
- Defile (Dirty, doing that are opposite of truth)
- Suicide (act of killing of self)
- Hostility (unfriendly, hostile act or resistance to an idea or plan)

In this subject, there are scriptures that help us to identify these attitudes or behaviors in our carnal way of thinking or acts.

Galatians 5:19-21 (Amplified Bible): 19Now the practices of the[a]sinful nature are clearly evident: they are sexual immorality, impurity, sensuality (total irresponsibility, lack of self-control),20 [b]idolatry,[c]sorcery, hostility, strife, jealousy, fits of anger, disputes, dissensions, factions [that promote heresies],21 envy, drunkenness, riotous behavior, and other things like these. I warn you beforehand, just as I did previously, that those who practice such things will not inherit the kingdom of God.

Chapter Seven: Being Transformed

How is one called to be set apart? How can one become an example of Christ? The scripture in Psalm 4:3 can tell us how God calls his chosen ones to become set apart from the world.

Psalm 4:3 (Amplified Bible): 3) But know that the LORD has set apart for Himself [and dealt wonderfully with] the godly man [the one of honorable character and moral courage—the one who does right]. The LORD hears and responds when I call to Him.

John 15:16-17 (Amplified Bible): 16 You have not chosen Me, but I have chosen you and I have appointed and placed and purposefully planted you, so that you would go and bear fruit and keep on bearing, and that your fruit will remain and be lasting, so that whatever you ask of the Father in My name [as My representative] He may give to you. 17 This [is what] I command you: that you love and unselfishly seek the best for one another.

How important is Self-Control in our transformation to having the Spiritual fruits of God? Galatians 5:22-23 (KJV): 22) But the fruit of the spirit is love, joy, peace, forbearance, kindness, goodness, faithfulness and self-control (self-restraint) –the ability to manage your actions, feelings and emotions), Against such things there is no law. 23) Meekness, temperance: against such there is no law.

Humility: Humility is a word we do not take to heart. However Jesus Christ demonstrated very well how we can become in his likeness to adapt to change for the good. He once died for all, that we can become a new creature in him. This is very important why? We can make a major change in our lives pleading for God's deliverance, healing and more of his loving presence. It starts with putting God first, You, family, friends, etc.

Romans 6:9-10 (Amplified Bible): [9]because we know [the self-evident truth] that Christ, having been raised from the dead, will never die again; death no longer has power over Him. [10]For the death that He died, He died to sin [ending its power and paying the sinner's debt] once and for all; and the life that He lives, He lives to [glorify] God [in unbroken fellowship with Him].

2 Corinthians 5:17-18 (Amplified Bible): [17]Therefore if anyone is in Christ [that is, grafted in, joined to Him by faith in Him as Savior], he is a new creature [reborn and renewed by the Holy Spirit]; the old things [the previous moral and spiritual condition] have passed away. Behold, new things have come [because spiritual awakening brings a new life]. [18]But all these things are from God, who reconciled us to Himself through Christ [making us acceptable to Him] and gave us the ministry of reconciliation [so that by our example we might bring others to Him],

Apostle Paul's writings of Christ Jesus about humility and how it is demonstrated clearly. We must accept the way that God is revealing to us that transformation is important in every Christian walk with the Lord in life. We should live by God's principles that will help strengthen our faith to be a living witness for him. I would like to share some more scriptures that will help define transformation as God's word makes it so perfectly clear to us.

Philippians 2:5-11 (Amplified Bible): [5]Have this same attitude in yourselves which was in Christ Jesus [look to Him as your example in selfless humility], [6]who, although He existed in the form and unchanging essence of God [as One with Him, possessing the fullness of all the divine attributes—the entire nature of deity], did not regard equality with God a thing to be grasped or asserted [as if He did not already possess it, or was afraid of losing it]; [7]but emptied Himself [without renouncing or diminishing His deity, but only temporarily giving up the outward expression of divine equality and His rightful dignity] by assuming the form of a bond-servant, and being made in the likeness of men [He became completely human but was without sin, being fully God and fully man].

[8]After He was found in [terms of His] outward appearance as a
man [for a divinely-appointed time], He humbled Himself [still further]
by becoming obedient [to the Father] to the point of death, even death
on a cross. [9]For this reason also [because He obeyed and so completely
humbled Himself], God has highly exalted Him and bestowed on Him
the name which is above every name, [10] so that at the name of Jesus
[a]EVERY KNEE SHALL BOW [in submission], of those who are in
heaven and on earth and under the earth, [11]and that every tongue will
confess and openly acknowledge that Jesus Christ is Lord (sovereign
God), to the glory of God the Father.

What a redemptive Savior Jesus Christ we have to receive a true relationship and fellowship with him! We can come to him empty, lost, broken hearted and in despair Jesus paid it all for us so that we can have this newness of life in him! He can only forgive us and cleanse us from our sinful ways. We have that wonderful assurance in him! Jesus Christ is our salvation! We can be safe, free and sealed up with the Holy Spirit my God today! What a mighty God we serve who can do all things but fail.

Chapter Eight: Am I Disciplined? The Church, You, and Me

I am excited to share this word of Revelation the Lord has revealed to me. Just think of the body and its functions in the natural being. But think of this way as the Body of Jesus Christ ought to function, becoming disciplined in him.

Head: God the Father, Son Jesus Christ and Holy Spirit: Is all one, the Trinity functioning together, you cannot leave one out without the other. Colossians 1:18-20 (Amplified Bible): 18 He is also the head [the life-source and leader] of the body, the [a]church; and He is the beginning, [b]the firstborn from the dead, so that He Himself will occupy the first place [He will stand supreme and be preeminent] in everything. 19 For it pleased the Father for all the fullness [of deity—the sum total of His essence, all His perfection, powers, and attributes] to dwell [permanently] in Him (the Son), 20 and through [the intervention of] the Son to reconcile all things to Himself, making peace [with believers] through the blood of His cross; through Him, [I say,] whether things on earth or things in heaven.

Eyes: Psalm 119:18 (Amplified Bible): Open my eyes [to spiritual truth] so that I may behold wonderful things from Your law.

Ears: Job 36:10 (Amplified Bible): He opens their ears to instruction and discipline, And commands that they return from evil.

Neck: 2 Samuel 22:41 (King James Version Bible): 41Thou hast also given me the necks of mine enemies, that I might destroy them that hate me.

Shoulders: Matthew 11:28-29 (Amplified Bible): 28 "Come to Me, all who are weary and heavily burdened [by religious rituals that provide no peace], and I will give you rest [refreshing your souls with salvation]. 29Take My yoke upon you and learn from Me [following Me as My disciple], for I am gentle and humble in heart, and YOU WILL FIND REST (renewal, blessed quiet) FOR YOUR SOULS.

Heart: Psalm 119: 11 (Amplified Bible): Your word I have treasured and stored in my heart, That I may not sin against You.

Mouth: Matthew 7:7 (Amplified Bible): 7 "[a]Ask and keep on asking and it will be given to you; seek and keep on seeking and you will find; knock and keep on knocking and the door will be opened to you.

Tongue: Pray without ceasing; 1 Thessalonians 5:17 (KJV)

Hands: Touch not; taste not; handle not: Colossians 2:21 (KJV), We must abstain from anything that is not profitable for us. Get rid of it!

Belly: But whosoever drinketh of the water that I shall give him shall never thirst, but the water that I shall give him shall be in him a well of water springing up into everlasting life. John 4:14 (KJV)

Arms/Hands: I will bless you as long as I live; I will lift up my hands in your name. Psalm 63:4 (KJV)

Legs: That ye might walk worthy of thee LORD unto all pleasing, being fruitful in every good work and increasing in the knowledge of God. Colossians 1:10 (KJV)

I want to unfold this revelation as we are born again believers in Jesus Christ as " his church," we must demonstrate how to become self-disciplined in our spiritual walk in our journey with the LORD. It is important to be partakers of the sufferings of Jesus Christ. How can one become disciplined? How can we become mature in Christ? How can an overcomer in Jesus Christ face circumstances in our lives? How can our faith become strengthened? How can we become delivered by the power of darkness? How can we be redeemed from our sinful nature? What a mighty God we serve!

Romans 7:24 King James Version (KJV): 24 O wretched man that I am! who shall deliver me from the body of this death. We have to acknowledge we are a wretched person and only Christ can redeem us from the power of darkness and our sinful nature, that we can be transformed in the likeness of Jesus Christ.

Deliverance: Who hath delivered us from the power of darkness, and hath translated us into the kingdom of his dear son. Colossians 4:13 (KJV).

Redemption: In whom we have redemption through his blood, even the forgiveness of sins. Colossians 4:14 (KJV).

Chapter Nine: Healing to Become Self-Disciplined

Healing: How can we learn to let go and to accept the fullness of what God has promised us? How can we let go of our past, the trauma and the horrific things that have happened to us? Healing is defined to be made whole, complete and a need to be restored. How can one know that he or she is healed? Can evidence show that this is really true? Can one overcome any social, mental, physical conditions in their life? The answer is "Yes" it is possible according to one's faith to believe! God is able to heal us, if we accept him, and believe he can do what man cannot demonstrate to do by his supernatural power.

Therefore, we must desire God's healing for our life, we must examine ourselves, acknowledge that there is a need for healing. We must learn to forgive; it is a major part of the healing process. We must have a willingness to be restored by creating a positive atmosphere around you. Transformation, determination and Mutation is very important during the stages of healing in our lives. We must let go of fear and self-rejection, learn from the lessons in life to help benefit you to grow, shape us into the person God intended for us to become. How can I say that, yes we have cried, yes we were hurt so badly that lowered our self-esteem, yes we have put ourselves in compromising situations that should have never happened.

This is a part that we can become nurtured in overcoming these obstacles to have that win, win attitude to say I can do this! The painting process is for someone else you went through. You survived, you made it, but you didn't stay damaged. It's for your story, for God's Glory! I would like to share a powerful scripture that can speak good and positive things in your life. I hope this will empower you in such a way, that nothing will not be able to stand in your way.

I would like to share gem sayings of wisdom that will both empower and enlighten you!

1. Kind words that you speak into your life will bring greater results
2. With God all things are possible
3. Walk by faith, not by sight
4. Surrender to God wholeheartedly
5. Pray earnestly to desire God more

Healing Scriptures

Proverbs 16:24 Amplified Bible (AMP): 24 Pleasant words are like a honeycomb, Sweet and delightful to the soul and healing to the body.

Jeremiah 33:6 Amplified Bible (AMP): 6Behold, [in the restored Jerusalem] I will bring to it health and healing, and I will heal them; and I will reveal to them an abundance of peace (prosperity, security, stability) and truth.

Luke 9:11 Amplified Bible (AMP): 11But when the crowds learned of it, they followed Him; and He welcomed them and He began talking to them about the kingdom of God, and healing those who needed to be healed.

A Prayer of Healing by the Prophet Jeremiah:

Jeremiah 17:14 Amplified Bible (AMP): 14 Heal me, O LORD, and I will be healed; Save me and I will be saved, For You are my praise.

Restoration plays a major important healing agent in one's life, to be brought back to life for deliverance and recovery. This word can be recognize as one is prepared for surgery to remove the plague or infirmity in one's body. We can imagine after going through this process, if the procedure is done correctly, there are instructions we have to follow to heal properly.

However, we may not always understand the many processes God takes us through. God is the master surgeon and we are his children, he knows exactly when we are in need of pruning and cultivating in our spiritual lives to be completely healed in the areas we are lacking in! Amen! In the restoration process, he is able to renew our mind, give us the peace in him, bring conviction in our hearts, purge us from our dark pasts and give us a new life through Christ.

King David in Psalm 51 is very instrumental and inspiring, even though the king fell into sin and became disobedient, God's judgment fell on David and David had common sense to acknowledge his secret faults and to ask God for forgiveness and to repent for his wrong-doings. King David earnestly seeks God for total restoration, covenant relationship with God. How he praises God for everything, and to reconcile back to God. I want to point out several verses that will encourage us all.

Psalm 51 Amplified Bible (AMP): 1)Have mercy on me, O God, according to Your lovingkindness; According to the greatness of Your compassion blot out my transgressions. 2) Wash me thoroughly from my wickedness and guilt And cleanse me from my sin. 3) For I am conscious of my transgressions and I acknowledge them; My sin is always before me. 10) Create in me a clean heart, O God, And renew a right and steadfast spirit within me. 12) Restore to me the joy of Your salvation and sustain me with a willing spirit. 15) O Lord, open my lips, That my mouth may declare Your praise.

Therefore, we must acknowledge our desire, for willingness to change for our goodness sake. Most importantly to accept God for his guidance, as he will help us to make the right decisions. Just note that progression does not always happen instantaneously. Unfortunate situations can be delayed, but not in God's denial, the plans and his purpose for you. Some healings that were recorded in God's word were instant to show the Glory of God and who he is that can resurrect us to believe, and that our faith will not fail in him! Jesus made a perfectly clear statement, to Thomas a disciple of Jesus, who didn't believe after Jesus was risen from the dead, the nails in his hands, piercing in his side, the beatings and lashings of the whip. Thomas doubted because he wanted to see how many of us were just like Thomas who became doubtful about what God's promises to us were. God is saying to us to believe and we are not to draw back into prediction. In spite of what you cannot see how God's hand is working in your life just simply BELIEVE!

John 20:28-30 Amplified Bible (AMP): 28 Thomas answered
Him, "My Lord and my God!" 29 Jesus said to him, "Because you have seen Me, do you now believe? Blessed [happy, spiritually secure, and favored by God] are they who did not see [Me] and yet believed Me]."

So imagine believing, yet not seeing will bless you of what miracle God tremendously does in your life!

30 There are also many other signs (attesting miracles) that Jesus performed in the presence of the disciples, which are not written
in this book; 31 but these have been written so that you may believe [with a deep, abiding trust] that Jesus is the Christ (the Messiah, the Anointed), the Son of God; and that by believing [and trusting in and relying on Him] you may have life in His name.

Believing through his name in all things produces change, improvement, restoration, growth and gratification.

Phase Two: Am I Disciplined?

In these several sessions I would like to explain these simple key elements that are very important to become self-disciplined:

Repentance
Trust
Honesty
Change
Willingness

Repentance is learning to admit your faults and transgressions (sins). Turn from your ways of wrongdoing and turn to our Father, the Lord Almighty. Transformational outlook in our daily lives must become effective in the healing process in learning how to let go and let God shape us in the way he intended us to be. The bible brings out unique teachings, how one must turn from its wrong doings and to seek God to ask for forgiveness. This is another way one can be free and healed from the temptation, dark secrets that are hidden within.

One good illustration in the bible is one of the disciples, Peter asks Jesus a question in Matthew 18:21-22. This passage is very familiar to us who do know it and still do not apply it to our lives daily! Amen! I would like to bring this bible verse to enlighten us as we will understand how to mature in our spiritual walk with Jesus. Matthew 18:21-22 Amplified Bible (AMP): Forgiveness [21] Then Peter came to Him and asked, "Lord, how many times will my brother sin against me and I forgive him and let it go? Up to seven times?" [22] Jesus answered him, "I say to you, not up to seven times, but seventy times seven. We must have forgiveness in our hearts, no matter what that individual has caused us, or how we allowed ourselves to get caught up in foolish situations."

We cannot take away from this principle how will our Heavenly Father forgive us, if we cannot not admit to the trespass? Repent to God, for he already knows all about it, nothing is withheld from the Father.

Hebrews 4:13 Amplified Bible (AMP): 13 And not a creature exists that is concealed from His sight, but all things are open and exposed, and revealed to the eyes of Him with whom we have to give account.

When we petition our prayers and requests to God, he loves when we can talk to him. It is important to acknowledge, admit and let go of what is keeping you from drawing close to the Father.

Another scripture explains why repentance is very important as God is speaking to us over and over again. Mark 1:15 Amplified Bible (AMP): 15 and saying, "The [appointed period of] time is fulfilled, and the kingdom of God is at hand; repent [change your inner self—your old way of thinking, regret past sins, live your life in a way that proves repentance; seek God's purpose for your life] and believe [with a deep, abiding trust] in the good news [regarding salvation]."

Acts 2:38 Amplified Bible (AMP): 38 And Peter said to them, "Repent [change your old way of thinking, turn from your sinful ways, accept and follow Jesus as the Messiah] and be baptized, each of you, in the name of Jesus Christ because of the forgiveness of your sins; and you will receive the gift of the Holy Spirit. Acts 3:19 Amplified Bible (AMP): 19 So repent [change your inner self—your old way of thinking, regret past sins] and return [to God—seek His purpose for your life], so that your sins may be wiped away [blotted out, completely erased], so that times of refreshing may come from the presence of the Lord [restoring you like a cool wind on a hot day];

Phase Two: Am I Disciplined?

Acts 2:38 (Amplified Bible): 38 And Peter said to them, "Repent [change your old way of thinking, turn from your sinful ways, accept and follow Jesus as the Messiah] and be baptized, each of you, in the name of Jesus Christ because of the forgiveness of your sins; and you will receive the gift of the Holy Spirit.

Trust: Trust is an important factor for many friendships, marriages and relationships are broken up by this simple word called "TRUST." We have lost our trust in GOD, and in one another. We must all put our trust in God is the main important necessity in our daily lives. It is unethical to think that you can do it without God in this journey, how are you going to do it without him? Because he is the main reason why you and I are here today. Many times in our humanism, we lose sight of what is important, we become burned out on having an interest in God and turn to other things that seem to excite us the most.

Who is the one who loves you first? When no one else told you that they loved you? Who ever knew your name before you did? Who kept you from destruction? Who was the one that cared so much for you when you have been rejected? Pushed aside? Hunger? And the list goes on! God cared so much for us, when we didn't trust anybody, simply because of hurt and turmoil. So we tend to build this wall around us not to trust anyone no more. It's sad to say when you don't trust yourself at all. Only God can heal your wounds and to erase those mental and physical scars in your life with a sincere heart.

Trust in God is the most valuable relationship with him. Leave the rest of your matters in his hands. As a firm believer he will help you and guide you in the right direction, if you trust him totally let him come into your heart. God will come in and dine with you. Let him speak to your heart, let him fill you with his Holy Spirit as he teaches you and lead you to all truth. He will, I'm a living witness. I have been scorned numerous times in my life. I can recall I have lost trust in myself and I trusted people so easily, simply I thought we were on the same page.

Ironically, this was not so the case. With that being said, when you establish your relationship with God, take notice that some people simply will not understand your journey with the LORD. In my case, I learned through many hard lessons, as a backslider and wanted to do what I wanted to do. It just didn't stop there. I had to commit myself back unto the Lord, to learn to trust again, especially in God first! So I urge you to repent, trust, believe and turn back to your first love God the Almighty, who the one created you, formed you out of your mother's womb!

Chapter Ten: Honesty: Am I Self- Disciplined?

Honesty is not relevant to some of us, we quite struggle within ourselves to go forward in being truthful. This is an important substance we must have to become the true church Jesus Christ has called us to be. This is one of the key elements that God has shared with me, when I began my walk with Jesus Christ during my conversion.

We must come to God with denial of self. Our desire for him should be in sincerity. God already knows our flaws; we cannot always use this as an excuse. He also knows our level of obedience. He already knows our actions, intentions and motives. There is nothing hidden from him that we cannot get away with. So as born again believers, Holy Ghost filled we must strive for honesty daily and to become more in the likeness of Jesus Christ. Jesus left us examples of how we must conduct ourselves and to behave in the house of God.

I would like to share with you a few scriptures that state how we must be willing to become honest. Romans 13:13-14 Amplified Bible (AMP): 13Let us conduct ourselves properly and honorably as in the [light of] day, not in carousing and drunkenness, not in sexual promiscuity and irresponsibility, not in quarreling and jealousy. 14But clothe yourselves with the Lord Jesus Christ and make no provision for [nor even think about gratifying] the flesh in regard to its improper desires.

John 15:4-11 Amplified Bible (AMP): 4Remain in Me, and I [will remain] in you. Just as no branch can bear fruit by itself without remaining in the vine, neither can you [bear fruit, producing evidence of your faith] unless you remain in Me. 5 [a]I am the Vine; you are the branches. The one who remains in Me and I in him bears much fruit, for [otherwise] apart from Me [that is, cut off from vital union with Me] you can do nothing. 6 If anyone does not remain in Me, he is thrown out like a [broken off] branch, and withers and dies; and they gather such branches and throw them into the fire, and they are burned. 7 If you remain in Me and My words remain in you [that is, if we are vitally united and My message lives in your heart], ask whatever you wish and it will be done for you. 8 My Father is glorified and honored by this, when you bear much fruit, and prove yourselves to be My [true] disciples. 9 I have loved you just as the Father has loved Me; remain in My love [and do not doubt My love for you]. 10 If you keep My commandments and obey My teaching, you will remain in My love, just as I have kept My Father's commandments and remain in His love. 11 I have told you these things so that My joy and delight may be in you, and that your joy may be made full and complete and overflowing. Amen!

Chapter Eleven: Change: Am I Disciplined?

Change is something we must learn how to make improvements and adjustments in our lives. How can one become better? How can one approve its ability, adapt to growth, dependency and maximize potential in transforming to overcome insecurities slipups? How can one improve? Why stay strung on being stuck? How do you react to the state of being uneased? How do you face opposition? How do you get from one stage to another? These are thoughts that have come across our minds at one point or another.

Some of us like to be content in just doing the same ole lame duck. We tend to stay in marble lanes for a long time. God is calling us to transform or change our mind set. We are comfortable with living in the past instead of the present. While being in the state of comfort zone instead of going beyond the breach from immaturity to maturity. I am reminded of the Apostle Paul who was telling the church of Corinthians about how to mature.

1 Corinthians 13:11 Amplified Bible (AMP): When I was a child, I talked like a child, I thought like a child, I reasoned like a child; when I became a man, I did away with childish things.

1 Corinthians 14:20 Amplified Bible (AMP): Instruction for the Church: [20] Brothers and sisters, do not be children [immature, childlike] in your thinking; be infants in [matters of] evil [completely innocent and inexperienced], but in your minds be mature [adults].

Please do not take this the wrong way, we do not realize how much time is wasted. We must grow on maturity. Do not let precious time pass you by. Have a different view of things in life, people, peers and our personal self being.

Change sometimes takes patience. The majority of us do not like to wait or become a patient person. How can we be used by God for his glory? If we are not willing to humble ourselves and desire for change? A wise saying, "There's always room for improvement." I shared a wisdom nugget long ago, "I shall not be bound by ignorance, but I shall grow in the wisdom of God"! Amen!

Oftentimes, God chases us from our errors, because of his genuine love for us. Change is something we must not take lightly; we must take it to heart. Change is to help us keep guarded to be geared in the right direction in having a genuine relationship with the LORD.

Job 14:14 Amplified Bible (AMP): "If a man dies, will he live again? I will wait all the days of my struggle until my change and release will come.

Chapter Twelve: Willingness: Am I Disciplined?

Willingness is listening very closely to wise instructions and piety in the things that are right. We must have a win, win attitude to become graciously eager to do what God has for us instead of the demand of mankind. Why is this important? Willingness in the mind, ability to endure in all areas in the learning process, relying on the Holy Spirit for revelation and confirmation. God is Holy, his word is perfect, God cannot lie in what he does.

We must have the mindset to do what is healthy, prudent, well-nourished and balanced lifestyle. It is imperative to think not at the things we do not have. We sometimes belittle ourselves by creating negative spaces. I would like to use this analogy; you do not wear the same clothes over twenty years and do not require to change your wardrobe, do you? We must be prompt to transformational ways to be an overcomer and not become overtaken by fear, failure and negativity.

2 Corinthians 8:12 Amplified Bible (AMP): 12 For if the eagerness [to give] is there, it is acceptable according to what one has, not according to what he does not have.

Why is this important? Do we have the right intentions? Do we take more than we give? Do we desire the needs more instead of God provision for our lives? Do we want to take charge over everything? Are you a subordinate helper for the Kingdom of God? It is all about you and not God? We need to change our mindsets the way we do things. The act of willingness, to do things without hesitation. Why is this important? Willingness in the mind, we must put into practice how to become focused on hearing and obeying the voice of God in everything in our life.

God delights in his people and every detail in their life. How is this possible with having a willing mind? Willingness requires an intimate relationship with God. One of the prerequisites is to know him and who he is. We quite lack this area in our walk with the Lord. Do we truly know him? Or have we heard of him?

Be willing to lay aside every weight in your life that is separating you from God. Willingness is necessary to stay focused on the Lord, yes distractions come and go. Keep your eyes on him, temptation preys, your eyes on him. We must adapt to making positive changes and do it with humility. God is the only one who can give us peace in our mind. God's plan is perfect and is accurate. We can make room for improvement and spiritual maturity.

I would like to share a few stories of how Jesus demonstrated his love for the Father and his willingness, having compassion on the people. The story of Phillip, the Evangelist with the Ethiopian servant, his conversion to Christ and how he was willing to follow Jesus. Willingness is without hesitation, just do it without second guessing is this God? Or is it just my imagination?

Jesus' willingness to humble himself as a servant in washing the disciples' feet. John 13:5-16 Amplified Bible (AMP): 5 Then He poured water into the basin and began washing the disciples' feet and wiping them with the towel which was tied around His waist. 6 When He came to Simon Peter, he said to Him, "Lord, are You going to wash my feet?" 7 Jesus replied to him, "You do not realize now what I am doing, but you will [fully] understand it later."

8 Peter said to Him, "You will never wash my feet!" Jesus answered, "Unless I wash you, you have no part with Me [we can have nothing to do with each other]." 9 Simon Peter said to Him, "Lord, [in that case, wash] not only my feet, but also my hands and my head!" 10 Jesus said to him, "Anyone who has bathed needs only to wash his feet, and is completely clean. And you [My disciples] are clean, but not all of you." 11

For He knew who was going to betray Him; for that reason He said, "Not all of you are clean."

12 So when He had washed their feet and put on His [outer] robe and reclined at the table again, He said to them, "Do you understand what I have done for you? 13 You call Me Teacher and Lord, and you are right in doing so, for that is who I am. 14 So if I, the Lord and the Teacher, washed your feet, you ought to wash one another's feet as well. 15 For I gave you [this as] an example, so that you should do [in turn] as I did to you. 16 I assure you and most solemnly say to you, a slave is not greater than his master, nor is one who is sent greater than the one who sent him.

Jesus' willingness showed without hesitation his concern of others, instead of himself for his love of the Father and the people. Jesus' willingness to heal the man with Leprosy and the man's willingness to be healed. Matthew 8:1-4 Amplified Bible (AMP): 8 When Jesus came down from the mountain, large crowds followed Him. 2 And a leper came up to Him and bowed down before Him, saying, "Lord, if You are willing, You are able to make me clean (well)." 3 Jesus reached out His hand and touched him, saying, "I am willing; be cleansed." Immediately his leprosy was cleansed. 4 And Jesus said to him, "See that you tell no one [about this]; but go, show yourself to the priest [for inspection] and present the offering that Moses commanded, as a testimony (evidence) to them [of your healing]."

Phillip the Evangelist and the Ethiopian Servant

The Ethiopian servant's willingness to become converted and to give his life to Jesus Christ. Acts 8:26-40 Amplified Bible (AMP): 26 But an angel of the Lord said to Philip, "Get up and go south to the road that runs from Jerusalem down to Gaza." (This is a desert road). 27 So he got up and went; and there was an Ethiopian eunuch [a man of great authority], a court official of Candace, queen of the Ethiopians, who was in charge of all her treasure. He had come to Jerusalem to worship, 28 and he was returning, and sitting in his chariot he was reading [the scroll of] the prophet Isaiah.[29] Then the [Holy] Spirit said to Philip, "Go up and join this chariot."[30] Philip ran up and heard the man reading the prophet Isaiah, and asked, "Do you understand what you are reading?"[31]And he said, "Well, how could I [understand] unless someone guides me [correctly]?" And he invited Philip to come up and sit with him.[32]

Now this was the passage of Scripture which he was reading: "LIKE A SHEEP HE WAS LED TO THE SLAUGHTER; AND AS A LAMB BEFORE ITS SHEARERS IS SILENT, SO HE DOES NOT OPEN HIS MOUTH. [33] "IN HUMILIATION HIS JUDGMENT WAS TAKEN AWAY [justice was denied Him]. WHO WILL DESCRIBE HIS GENERATION? FOR HIS LIFE IS TAKEN FROM THE EARTH." [34] The eunuch replied to Philip, "Please tell me, about whom does the prophet say this? About himself or about someone else?"[35] Then Philip spoke and beginning with this Scripture he preached Jesus to him [explaining that He is the promised Messiah and the source of salvation].[36]As they continued along the road, they came to some water; and the eunuch exclaimed, "Look! Water! What forbids me from being baptized?"

37 [a][Philip said to him, "If you believe with all your heart, you may." And he replied, "I do believe that Jesus Christ is the Son of God."][38]And he ordered that the chariot be stopped; and both Philip and the eunuch went down into the water, and Philip baptized him.[39]When they came up out of the water, the Spirit of the Lord [suddenly] took Philip [and carried him] away [to a different place]; and the eunuch no longer saw him, but he went on his way rejoicing.[40] But Philip found himself at[b]Azotus, and as he passed through he preached the good news [of salvation] to all the cities, until he came to [c]Caesarea [Maritima].

How beautiful that each story is relative and shows how God can change your situations if you believe to have a willing acceptable mind in Jesus Christ!

Impartation:

The defined term of self-discipline is: The ability you have to control and motivate yourself to stay on track and to do what is right. In these next chapters I will explain these following terms are important for the church, our leaders that are in leadership, and us who are determined to do what it takes to become self-control in Jesus Christ!

Self-Control
Rightful Cause
Forgiving

These areas will help one to become effective and will overcome many obstacles through the word of God, you would not think to let go of! Amen! In this chapter, I would like to share a word of Revelation and scriptures that will help define your purpose in God with how we must submit ourselves to God as he leads us the way in every aspect of our life. Self-Control: the ability to manage your actions, feelings and emotions. Learning to refrain from habits that are not healthy for us in general. We must abstain from negative thoughts or actions.

Self-Control in the Church Women:
1 Timothy 3:11 Amplified Bible: 11 [d]Women must likewise be worthy of respect, not malicious gossip, but self-controlled, [thoroughly] trustworthy in all things.

Self-Control in the Church Men:
1 Timothy 3:8-10 Amplified Bible: 8 Deacons likewise must be men worthy of respect [honorable, financially ethical, of good character], not double-tongued [speakers of half-truths], not addicted to wine, not greedy for dishonest gain, 9 but upholding and fully understanding the mystery [that is, the true doctrine] of the [Christian] faith with a clear conscience [resulting from behavior consistent with spiritual maturity]. 10 These men must first be tested; then if they are found to be blameless and beyond reproach [in their Christian lives], let them serve as deacon.

Leadership in the Church:
2 Peter 1:6-7 Amplified Bible: 6 and in your knowledge, self-control, and in your self-control, steadfastness, and in your steadfastness, godliness, 7 and in your godliness, brotherly affection, and in your brotherly affection, [develop Christian] love [that is, learn to unselfishly seek the best for others and to do things for their benefit].

However, another important factor is how Leaders must be self-disciplined:

Integrity: Honesty and having a desire to be unified in the state of mind, in decision making and choosing the right path to go. Leaders must refrain from having a divided state of mind and not feeding into negativity.

Direct: straight forwardness, narrow your focus and to be specific of how important the needs are in the congregation of the church God has commissioned you at.

Responsibility: One must be reliable , trustworthy of actions that are accountable for what's legal in a rightful matter.

2 Timothy 1:9 (Amplified Bible): 9 for He delivered us and saved us and called us with a holy calling [a calling that leads to a consecrated life—a life set apart—a life of purpose], not because of our works [or because of any personal merit—we could do nothing to earn this], but

because of His own purpose and grace [His amazing, undeserved favor] which was granted to us in Christ Jesus before the world began [eternal ages ago].

This is an important and serious calling God has given to those he has chosen for his elect, not by man say, "You ought to be like so and so," nor by tradition we shall not be placed in something we were not called to do! God has who he chose before we were ever created before we ever existed. Amen!

God Chooses:

Ephesians 1:4-5 Amplified Bible: 4 Just as [in His love] He chose us in Christ [actually selected us for Himself as His own] before the foundation of the world, so that we would be holy [that is, consecrated, set apart for Him, purpose-driven] and blameless in His sight. In love 5 He predestined and lovingly planned for us to be adopted to Himself as [His own] children through Jesus Christ, in accordance with the kind intention and good pleasure of His will.

Matthew 22:14 Amplified Bible: 14 For many are called (invited, summoned), but few are chosen."

Phillipians 1:6 Amplified Bible: 6 I am convinced and confident of this very thing, that He who has begun a good work in you will [continue to] perfect and complete it until the day of Christ Jesus [the time of His return].

In this next chapter will be a very brief insight on Rightful Cause. These two words are defined in this order: Rightful: Fair, Just, Right Cause: Anyone or anything that brings about a result. When you can put these two words together, what comes to mind is to change one's self or make the right decision that will bring an end to a good result. You may ask this question "Why is this important to become self-disciplined? Many of us have experienced making some wrongful decisions and unwise choices and in the end our plans have failed. However, we must learn from our mistakes and be willing to let go of all past faults.

We should become more tolerant of the things on how we can become self-controlled in our actions, morals and values.

I would like to share a story about my personal experience on the subject and I pray that this will enlighten you as you become self-disciplined. One of the hardest things for me to do is to let go. Meaning I had to take full responsibility to become disciplined in things God has told me " yes or no" to. I have found myself at times disobeying the voice of God, which lead to hard lessons and consequences. The more intense the trials were, the more I've struggled. I had to make a completely rightful decision with God's help to say enough is enough with people who I didn't realize took advantage of my kindness and kept me captive because of the gift of God upon my life. I am no longer I but the Christ that lives within me. I was once homeless living house to house, giving more of my talents, time and money to people who were not supportive for my sake and well-being.

Allow me to explain this a lot further. I thought I was doing the right thing by helping others, later I found out they didn't have any concerns for me. I was faced with debt problems. I had to take on other responsibilities that I was kind hearted to do. I was helping to make their ends meet, instead of making my ends meet. Later on as years passed by, when God told me to get away from certain individuals, I got away from them immediately! Later as years passed by, I was not aware of people using my private information, unbeknownst to me I was not aware of this kind of foolishness! This is just not right at all! I had to endure some painful nights, restless moments, and was quite often faced with rejection. This weight took a toll on my health, well-being and welfare.

I had to learn from these situations to yield and surrender all things to GOD. I had to learn to say "No" to a lot of things, this is how GOD was breaking me from this environment and emotional bondage cycle. It took a faithful, loving, GOD to make me rethink things over. By GOD teaching and showing me how to become self-disciplined of my actions, my behavior and maintaining my health and proper planning.

However, in decision making there is a such thing of having a rightful cause, even when one thinks it's not necessary. I believe it is important in any given situation to have positive thinking. There are times we may think quickly in making our decision right then and there. It takes good moral support to help us make the right choices in life that will bring a good result at the end of a matter. Trust and believe GOD will help us to define every purpose and plan he has intended for us to wit, experience and to endure that will become fruitful in our lives.

Although take legal action to stand up for what is right. Take a stand in what is truth and to know how to overcome these obstacles that have tried to weigh us down. Yes there will be moments that can become stressful, be we cannot afford to let the stress rule or reign over our lives. Take full action to think of good things, we can make it, it will get better with God's hands upon our lives. I hope and pray that these words will help and encourage you in times like these. I like to also encourage you with the word of God, as it relates to a willing mind.

1 Chronicles 28:9 Amplified Bible (AMP): 9)"As for you, Solomon my son, know the God of your father [have personal knowledge of Him, be acquainted with, and understand Him; appreciate, heed, and cherish Him] and serve Him with a blameless heart and a willing mind; for the Lord searches all hearts and minds, and understands every intent and inclination of the thoughts. If you seek Him [inquiring for and of Him and requiring Him as your first and vital necessity] He will let you find Him; but [a]if you abandon (turn away from) Him, He will reject you forever. Amen!

It takes God to grant us how we must serve him, our hearts must be blameless, our minds must be willing! Nothing is hidden from God he knows our thoughts; he searches all hearts and minds, and he sees everything! We must seek him and he will be found, If we seek him not, he will withdraw himself from us! God is our only hope and God cannot lie in what he has for us, and that he promised us that he will do! If we believe and trust him totally. Nothing cannot come past the GOD period! What a mighty GOD we serve! Amen!

Self-Disciplined "Learning to Forgive"

Forgiveness is a perfect illustration that represents Christ's Deity. We as Christians, men, women, boys, and girls, must learn how to forgive. Even though this is a hard thing to do, especially what has been done to us in times past. The best way that we can define the term "forgiveness" is: Forgiveness is the act of pardoning an offender. In the Bible, the Greek word translated "forgiveness" literally means "to let go," as when a person does not demand payment for a debt. Jesus used this comparison when he taught his followers to pray: "Forgive us our sins, for we ourselves also forgive everyone who is in debt to us." We must forgive daily; we should have an open heart to receive God's total healing to restore the broken pieces in our lives. Forgive yourself in order to forgive others, how can your Heavenly Father forgive you if you cannot forgive others?

Matthew 6:12 (Amplified Bible): 'And forgive us our [g]debts, as we have forgiven our debtors [letting go of both the wrong and the resentment].

Matthew 6:15-16 (Amplified Bible): 14 For if you forgive [k]others their trespasses [their reckless and willful sins], your heavenly Father will also forgive you. 15 But if you do not forgive others [nurturing your hurt and anger with the result that it interferes with your relationship with God], then your Father will not forgive your trespasses.

Why is this important to becoming self-disciplined?

1. It is a requirement by God, we must forgive men for their trespass, then your Heavenly Father will forgive you for your trespass.

2. It teaches us if we desire to follow Christ to have an intimate relationship with him.

3. We must die to our fleshly nature in order to seek God, receive the Holy Spirit, pray earnestly, and to study God's word.

4. We must demonstrate good productivity if we desire to become effective in serving God and the plans he has for our lives.

5. We must take full responsibility for our actions and admit our mistakes.

6. We can break this cycle in learning how to forgive and letting it go for our good! I would like to share some scriptures that will enlighten all of us, some can relate to it more than others!

John Chapter Eight gives a clear example how Jesus forgave the woman who was brought in the temple court, was caught in the act of adultery and how the rulers were trying to accuse Jesus in an act. We have experienced a similar situation in our lives when we were caught up in an act. People who falsely accused you of something you didn't do. When you mature in Christ, you will have people who will discredit you, by God's gift and the ability he placed inside of you to be a witness for him for his people. But when enduring this type of persecution, we must learn how to forgive to be forgiven.

John 8:1-11 (New King James Version) But Jesus went to the Mount of Olives.

2 Now [a]early in the morning He came again into the temple, and
all the people came to Him; and He sat down and taught them. 3 Then
the scribes and Pharisees brought to Him a woman caught in adultery.
And when they had set her in the midst, 4 they said to Him, "Teacher,
[b]this woman was caught in adultery, in the very act. 5 Now [c]Moses,
in the law, commanded us [d]that such should be stoned. But what do
You [e]say?" 6 This they said, testing Him, that they might have something of which to accuse Him. But Jesus stooped down and wrote on the ground with His finger, [f]as though He did not hear.

7 So when they continued asking Him, He [g]raised Himself up and
said to them, "He who is without sin among you, let him throw a stone
at her first." 8 And again He stooped down and wrote on the ground. 9
Then those who heard it, being[h] convicted by their conscience, went

out one by one, beginning with the oldest even to the last. And Jesus was left alone, and the woman standing in the midst. 10 When Jesus had raised Himself up [i]and saw no one but the woman, He said to her, "Woman, where are those accusers [j]of yours? Has no one condemned you?" 11 She said, "No one, Lord." And Jesus said to her, "Neither do I condemn you; go [k]and sin no more."

The Conclusion

Thank you for your participation in reading this book. I pray that you are encouraged and many revelations have poured into your spirit. Am I disciplined? What must I do to become self-controlled?

How to challenge myself to become disciplined? Learning how to let go and forgive. How to become transformed. What must I do to change my way of thinking? How must leadership become self-disciplined and we as the Church of Jesus Christ? How we must conduct ourselves in the house of God. How we as parents must show discipline in our homes, children and self. Being honest, knowing right from wrong. We must become mature saints in Jesus Christ for the world to see the light of Jesus Christ in us.

As I began to write this book years ago, I did not have a clue what God was doing in my life. I had to come into a place of perfect quietness in him. I have experienced hardships, afflictions in my body and frustrations along the way, But GOD! I did not have any intentions of thinking of writing a book so full of God's wisdom and his word! The Bible is all truth, without errors and is the most important book than any other book to be read. I cannot take any credit for this; it is all GOD! GOD from the beginning until the end of eternal life is all him!

I am no longer I, but it is the Christ that lives in me and he gave his life for me, and in return I give all that I have back to him. Without him I would not be where I am in this life. Amen! Jesus prays for his disciples and for us.

John 17:20-26 Amplified Bible (AMP): 20 "I do not pray for these
alone [it is not for their sake only that I make this request], but also for
[all] those who [will ever] believe and trust in Me through their message,21that they all may be one; just as You, Father, are in Me and I in

You, that they also may be one in Us, so that the world may believe [without any doubt] that You sent Me.

The Future Glory

22 I have given to them the glory and honor which You have given
Me, that they may be one, just as We are one; 23 I in them and You in Me,
that they may be perfected and completed into one, so that the world
may know [without any doubt] that You sent Me, and [that You] have
loved them, just as You have loved Me. 24 Father, I desire that they also,
whom You have given to Me [as Your gift to Me], may be with Me where
I am, so that they may see My glory which You have given Me, because
You loved Me before the foundation of the world. 25 "O just and righteous Father, although the world has not known You and has never ac-
knowledged You [and the revelation of Your mercy], yet I have always
known You; and these [believers] know [without any doubt] that You
sent Me; 26 and I have made Your name known to them, and will continue to make it known, so that the love with which You have loved Me
may be in them [overwhelming their heart], and I [may be] in them."

2 Peter 3:18 Amplified Bible (AMP): 18 but grow [spiritually mature] in the grace and knowledge of our Lord and Savior Jesus Christ. To Him be glory (honor, majesty, splendor), both now and to the day of eternity. Amen.

Poem of Discipline:
I must move on
I must move forward
I must become forgiving and forsaking the terrible.
I must stay active in doing what's right.
I must trust God at all times.
When challenging situations come I must be steadfast in God.
I must have a winning attitude.

Am I Disciplined?

I must be self-controlled at zero tolerance.
I must maintain and strive to have a balanced life in God.
I can do all things through Christ who strengthens me.
The one and only; who can lead me every
step along the way.
Oftentimes I may stray.
I'm confident that the Lord is my help.
I can truly say I'm kept.
Knowing in Jesus I have a true friend.

www.ingramcontent.com/pod-product-compliance
Lightning Source LLC
LaVergne TN
LVHW010121170826
845678LV00012B/2527

* 9 7 9 8 8 8 6 8 3 3 8 6 7 *